W9-BLD-754

WHAT DOGS DO, TOO

Photographs by Sharon Beals

CHRONICLE BOOKS

SAN FRANCISCO

**TO ALL OF THE DOGS WE SHARE OUR LIVES WITH.
WHERE WOULD WE BE WITHOUT THEM?**

Text copyright © 2002 by Sharon Beals.

Photographs copyright © 2002 by Sharon Beals.

Library of Congress Cataloging-in-Publication Data:

Beals, Sharon, 1945–
What dogs do, too / photographs by Sharon Beals.
p. cm.
ISBN 0-8118-3587-1
 1. Dogs—Pictorial works. 2. Photography of dogs. I. Title.
SF430 .B374 2002
636.7'0022'2—dc21
2001007117

Manufactured in China.

Book and cover design: Jessica Grunwald

Distributed in Canada by Raincoast Books
9050 Shaughnessy Street
Vancouver, BC V6P 6E5

10 9 8 7 6 5 4 3 2 1

Chronicle Books LLC
85 Second Street
San Francisco, California 94105

www.chroniclebooks.com

AND WE ONLY CALL THEM DOG

Sometimes just a glance at a dog can slam my heart—that visual thrill of coat and color, spots and marks, lash and whisker. It's a great feeling, sent both ways by a nudge of damp nose and a ruffle of fur, the name called and a sincere wag in answer; a mutuality expressed as often as honeymooners kiss.

Of course, there can be a few bumps of uncertainty: the shoe episodes, the upholstery incidents, for instance. And the design flaw of a dog's life span can make the heart-pulling even more poignant. But these drawbacks are far outweighed by dogs' perennial pupness, which makes them the best combination of friend, confidant, and comic. Even when they are gray-muzzled and moving slowly, they seem to be always wowing at the now, waving optimistic tails at life's next possibility. Their always-for-the-first-time glee over the bone, the walk, the car, the cat, mends my mood faster than any medicine or mantra. But you know that this dogness is not all play and no work. While they are rejuvenating our inner juvenile, they just happen to be using some senses that you and I will never get a whiff of knowing, practicing skills that can find the missing, know the way, or lead the blind.

If this sounds like the conviction of the saved, it is; and I'm not apologetic, only grateful. When I began snapping pictures of our world—people like you and me, people rarely seen without a canine capering at our heels—I thought: interesting slice of life. But I was sure everyone had all lost a few nuts to the squirrels.

Fortunately, the pictures made me so happy that I became a voyeur of these goodwill ambassadors long enough to know to say yes to the first stray that wandered into my life. An easy gentle soul, content with a regular meal and glad of my company, Sally stuck around long enough to make me weep hard for days when she eventually left to sniff her heavenly garbage cans.

Now the signs of my conversion are obvious, even if you haven't seen me driving around with that thirteen-pound muttlette in my lap: furry clothes, pockets full of treats, car windows totally nose-slimed. Oh, I still wear a little cat hair along with the fur, but the thought of life without the company of a dog can bring me to near panic. And I wouldn't trade this state of mind for anything.

MUSE

COOPERATE

MOPE

PESTER

LOVE

JIG

FETCH

SUFFER

CONFER

GROW

INDULGE

GO

OBSESS

PARTY

PERFORM

CAPER

UNDERSTAND

HARMONIZE

JEST

PINE

SEDUCE

MOSEY

ACCESSORIZE

FLY

VISIT

TRIUMPH

TUG

HANKER

DELIGHT

ACKNOWLEDGMENTS

I want to thank all of the big-hearted dogs I've known: my childhood dog, Vaughn, who literally saved my life; Lulu, surrogate dog and excellent traveler; Pete and Abe; sweet Sally; Chester and Pumpkin (who I have a crush on); and last and most importantly, the little muttlette at my side.

I have no end of gratitude to, and admiration for, Lynne Tingle at the Milo Foundation for her work rescuing dogs and cats whose time was up at the shelter. Many of these pets have made their appearance in my books and do again in this one. I am grateful to every person who has let me have my photographic way with their companions. And once again, to all of my friends and peers who help me with good opinions while I am making a book.